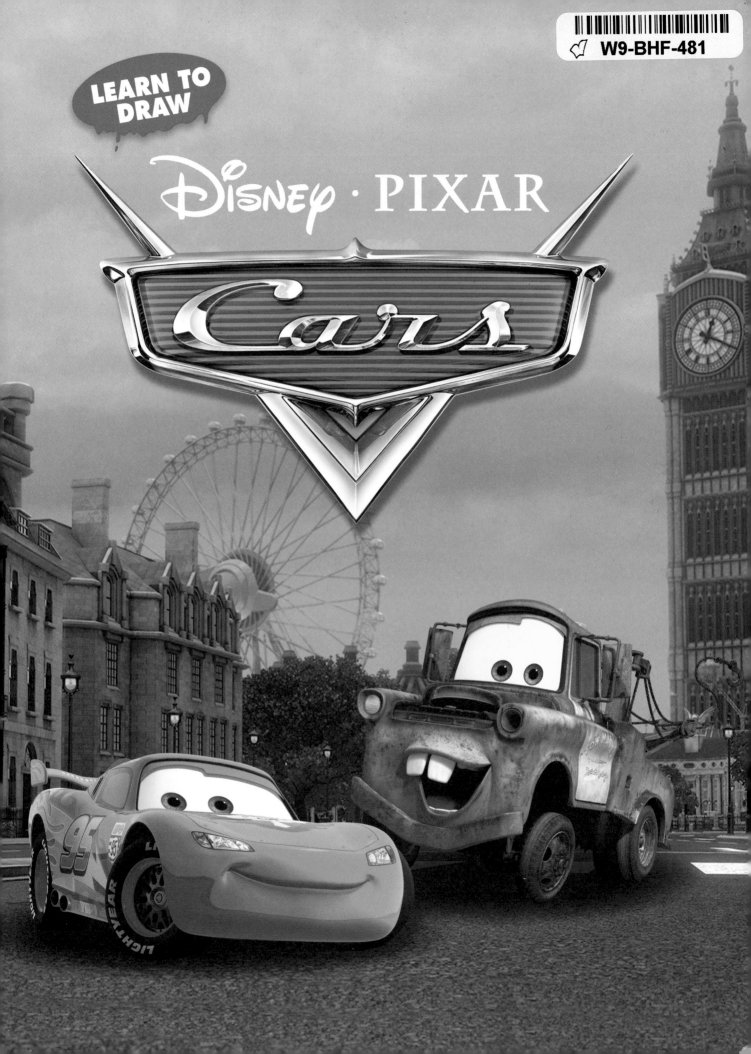

LEARN TO DRAW

Disney · PIXAR

Cars

LEARN TO DRAW

Disney · PIXAR

Cars

Illustrated by the Disney Storybook Artists, Marianne Tucker, and Andy Phillipson
Inspired by the character designs created by Pixar Animation Studios

Walter Foster

Table of Contents

It's time for the biggest car race of the year, the Dinoco 400. In this world, cars are the characters, and rookie sensation Lightning McQueen rolls out of his trailer to swarming reporters and cheering fans.

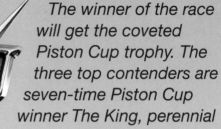

The winner of the race will get the coveted Piston Cup trophy. The three top contenders are seven-time Piston Cup winner The King, perennial runner-up Chick Hicks, and new hotshot Lightning McQueen. And with The King retiring, his lucrative Dinoco sponsorship is also up for grabs.

Lightning takes the lead! But at his pit stop, he refuses to change tires to save time. It's a bad move. In the final lap, his rear tires blow! Chick and The King catch up, and the race is too close to call!

While they wait for the results, The King tells Lightning he needs to treat his pit crew better, but Lightning isn't listening. He's daydreaming about his future glory . . . until he learns the race was a three-way tie! A tie-breaker race will be held in California in one week.

Reluctantly Lightning makes a quick appearance for Rust-eze, his current sponsor. Then he backs

wildly. He tears up the asphalt street and ends up hanging between two telephone poles.

The next morning, Lightning wakes up in the town impound. The Sheriff orders the friendly, rusty tow truck named Mater to tow Lightning to traffic court.

In court, Sally, the town's attorney, argues that the ruined road will turn away desperately needed customers. Doc, the judge, sentences Lightning to stay until he fixes the road.

Lightning is hooked to the messy paver named Bessie. After an hour he says he's finished, but the road looks terrible. Doc challenges Lightning to a race. If Lightning wins, he can go. But if Lightning loses, he will have to stay and finish the road Doc's way.

into his trailer and hits the road with his driver, Mack. Lightning pushes Mack to drive through the night. He wants to be the first to reach the California race. After many long hours, Mack dozes off. He swerves and Lightning falls out of the trailer!

Terrified, Lightning dodges the oncoming traffic and desperately follows Mack down an off-ramp—only to find it isn't Mack he was following! Lost and panicked, Lightning speeds through the small town of Radiator Springs. The Sheriff takes chase, making backfire noises that sound like gunshots, causing Lightning to drive

When the race begins, Lightning leaves Doc in the dust, speeding ahead and ripping around a turn . . . right over the edge of a deep ditch and into a cactus patch.

7

That night Lightning goes back to work. By morning, there is a beautiful, newly paved stretch of road.

Doc finds Lightning back at the dirt track trying to get the turn he missed. He tells Lightning that if he races on dirt and wants to turn left, sometimes he should steer right. Lightning laughs at the advice, but when no one is watching he tries it . . . and falls right into the cactus patch again.

The townsfolk are inspired by the new stretch of road, so they begin fixing up their shops. That night, Mater takes Lightning tractor tipping. And Lightning is having fun until a combine chases them off!

Back in town, Sally overhears Lightning explaining that winning the Piston Cup means he'll have fame, fortune, and a big new sponsor. He even promises Mater a helicopter ride. Thrilled, Mater declares Lightning his best friend.

Later Sally approaches Lightning and asks if he intends to keep his promise to Mater. Folks in Radiator Springs trust one another, and she doesn't want Mater to get hurt. The next morning, Lightning wanders into Doc's back office, where he finds three

THE NEXT MORNING, MATER AWAKENS THE WHOLE TOWN TO SHOW THEM THAT THE ROAD IS FINISHED. THEN LIGHTNING GOES SHOPPING—AND HE BECOMES THE BEST CUSTOMER RADIATOR SPRINGS HAS SEEN IN A LONG TIME.

Piston Cups and realizes that Doc is The Fabulous Hudson Hornet! Doc is furious that Lightning has discovered his secret, and he angrily shoos away Lightning.

Sally invites Lightning on a drive up the mountain. At the top, Sally tells the story of how she left Los Angeles and found her home in Radiator Springs. She also explains how Radiator Springs was bypassed when the Interstate was built. She'd give anything to have seen it in its heyday.

Later, Lightning secretly watches Doc gracefully racing at the dirt track. When Doc discovers Lightning, he leaves—but Lightning follows him. Doc finally lets out his secret: When he returned to the racing world after recovering from a big wreck, Doc was replaced by a rookie like Lightning McQueen.

The next morning, Mater awakens the whole town to show them that the road is finished. Then Lightning goes shopping—and he becomes the best customer Radiator Springs has seen in a long time. Sally is touched that Lightning helped all the townsfolk. As dusk settles, Lightning

cues the townsfolk to turn on their newly repaired neon lights. Radiator Springs is just like it was in its heyday. Everyone cruises happily.

But the mood is crushed by an invasion of reporters. Lightning has been found! Mack arrives to take Lightning to the big race. Lightning finds Sally in the crowd. Speechless, he listens to her as she wishes him luck. Then he sadly drives into the trailer and leaves.

The tie-breaker race is set to begin. Inside his trailer, Lightning tries to prepare, but his heart isn't in it. As the race begins, Lightning falls far behind . . . until he realizes all his pals from Radiator Springs have come to be his pit crew!

Newly determined, Lightning catches up with the leaders. His pit crew takes care of him and fixes a blown tire. And when Chick bumps into him, he quickly recovers by using the dirt-turn trick Doc taught him. Soon he pulls into first place!

When Chick causes The King to crash behind him, Lightning hears the crowd gasp and looks up at the stadium screen. The image reminds him of Doc's crash. Lightning slams on his brakes just before the finish line.

Chick wins the race but no one cares. Lightning reverses and pushes The King to a second-place finish and the crowd goes wild.

Lightning is offered the Dinoco sponsorship! But Lightning decides to stay with the loyal guys from Rust-eze.

He does ask Dinoco for one small favor, though: a helicopter ride for his friend Mater.

Alone on the mountain, Sally looks out over the valley when Lightning surprises her. He says he's opening up his headquarters in town. Their romantic moment is interrupted as Mater appears in the helicopter, singing. Sally laughs and tears off down the mountain. Lightning chases her. There's nowhere else he'd rather be.

Finn McMissile, a slick car on a secret mission, is spying on a criminal named Professor Z on an oil derrick in the middle of the Pacific ocean. He's about to uncover a convoluted plot when he's spotted by Gremlins and Pacers—the "Lemons." They chase Finn and destroy him—or so they think. Finn escapes unharmed.

Back in Radiator Springs, Lightning McQueen is fresh off his win at the Hudson Hornet Memorial Piston Cup Race. During dinner, Lightning's attention turns to the T.V. Italian race car Francesco Bernoulli is taunting Lightning, daring him to compete in the World Grand Prix sponsored by Miles Axlerod and his alternative fuel, Allinol. Lightning rises to the challenge, and "Team Lightning McQueen" heads to Tokyo for the first leg of the race.

In Tokyo at a fancy World Grand Prix party, Finn McMissile and fellow British

Agent Holley Shiftwell are undercover, waiting to receive a top-secret device from American Agent Rod "Torque" Redline.

In Mater's excitement at the party, he appears to leak oil in front of Miles Axlerod—much to Lightning's horror. Lightning tells Mater he is embarrassing him and sends Mater to the bathroom to clean up. While Mater is inside a stall, two Lemons corner Torque in the bathroom. As Mater exits, Torque plants the device on him—but Mater doesn't know. Holley detects the device and mistakes Mater for

the American spy. She arranges a meeting with him, but Mater thinks they have a date!

Professor Z realizes that the device has been passed to Mater. He instructs his minions, Grem and Acer, to find the tow truck. On race day, the cars fill up with Allinol and hit the track. During the race, Grem and Acer aim Professor Z's special "camera" at an unsuspecting race car. The camera beam causes the Allinol to boil—and explode! Later, Axlerod defends Allinol and reassures the public that his fuel is completely safe.

Holley speaks to Mater on his headset and guides him out of the pit for his safety. Mater repeats Holley's instructions out loud, but Lightning thinks Mater is directing him on the racetrack. He follows Mater's "racing tips" and loses to Francesco. Lightning blames Mater. Saddened, Mater decides to head home.

At the airport, Holley and Finn intercept Mater. Holley locates and

opens the device to reveal a photograph of an old, gas-guzzling engine that they are not able to identify. Finn suggests visiting Tomber in Paris. If anyone can identify an engine, it's Tomber. The trio heads to Paris, but Tomber can't identify the engine. Mater tells them that the engine belongs to a Lemon. Tomber tells them that the four Lemon families have planned a Lemonhead meeting in Porto Corsa, Italy—where the second leg of the race will be. Finn, Holley, and Mater head to Italy hoping to get more information.

In Italy, Lightning meets Luigi's Uncle Topolino and tells him about the fight with Mater. Topolino reminds Lightning that best friends may fight, but it's important to make up fast. Lightning is filled with regret.

Meanwhile, Holley disguises Mater as a Lemon's tow truck and equips him with voice-activated spy gadgets. Mater sneaks into the meeting while Holley and Finn listen in. Someone is trying to make Allinol appear dangerous so that everyone will go back to using gasoline! Later, at the race, Grem and Acer blow up several more race cars with the camera.

At the meeting, Mater overhears Professor Z order the Lemons to kill Lightning. Mater tries to leave to warn Lightning, but the Lemons capture him and reveal that a bomb is planted in Lightning's pit. Mater breaks free and rushes off to find Lightning. But he soon realizes the bomb is attached to him. Only the voice of the one who activated it can deactivate it!

Lightning and Mater are reunited, but Mater tries to keep away from Lightning. He doesn't want his friend to get hurt if the bomb goes off. Lightning refuses to leave Mater. He wants to apologize.

Finn captures Professor Z, and Holley takes care of the Lemon goons. Finally, Mater understands who is behind the plot to destroy the race cars and defame Allinol. Mater hooks onto Lightning and deploys his rocket thrusters and parachute. Mater and Lightning fly over London and land

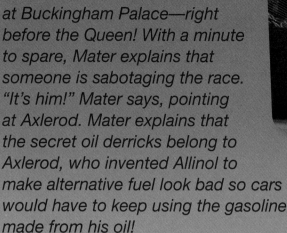

at Buckingham Palace—right before the Queen! With a minute to spare, Mater explains that someone is sabotaging the race. "It's him!" Mater says, pointing at Axlerod. Mater explains that the secret oil derricks belong to Axlerod, who invented Allinol to make alternative fuel look bad so cars would have to keep using the gasoline made from his oil!

With the bomb timer still ticking, Axlerod says, "Deactivate." The bomb stops— proving his guilt. His intention was to make all Lemons wealthy and powerful because they have lived in the shadows all their lives, being treated as second-rate cars. Because the Lemons own the majority of the world's oil, if all the cars went back to using gasoline, they would rely on the Lemons to supply their oil. Then the Lemons would finally get the respect they've waited so long for.

Mater is knighted by the Queen for uncovering the plot.

The gang heads back to Radiator Springs with all the race cars to finish the final leg of the race. Finn and Holley come too—they have a new assignment for Mater! But Mater politely declines. He is just fine where he is.

Tools & Materials

Ready, set, go! Lightning McQueen may require some fancy tools for a tune-up, but all you need to start drawing him—and all of his friends—are a few supplies. Use a pencil to get your drawing engine running. Then you can add color with felt-tip markers, colored pencils, watercolors, or acrylic paints. Ready to roll? *Ka-chow!*

drawing pencil and paper

colored pencils

paintbrush and paints

sharpener

eraser

felt-tip markers

Getting Started

Step 1

First draw the basic shapes.

Step 2

Each new step is shown in blue.

Step 3

Follow the blue lines to add the details.

Step 4

Now darken the lines you want to keep and erase the rest.

Add color!

15

Drawing Exercises

Warm up your hand by drawing lots of squiggles and shapes.

Draw a circle

Draw a square

Draw an oval

Draw a rectangle

Draw a triangle

If you can draw a few basic shapes, you can draw just about anything!

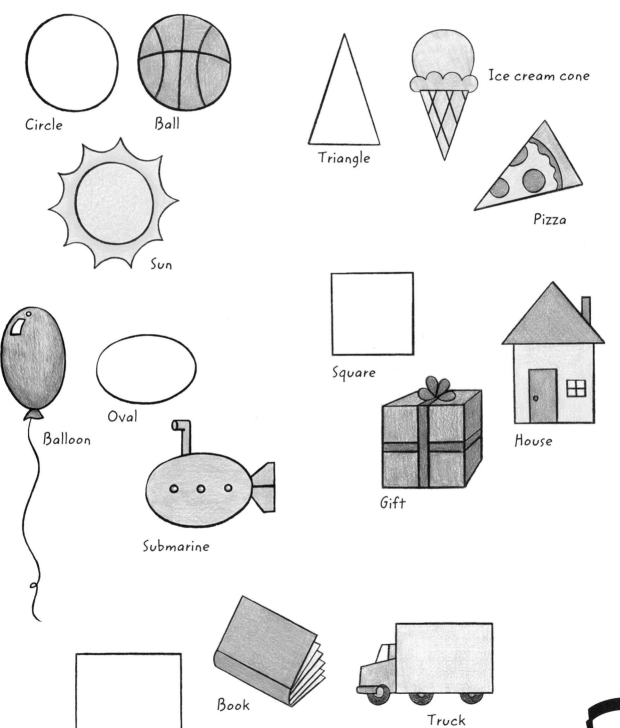

Circle

Ball

Triangle

Ice cream cone

Pizza

Sun

Square

House

Balloon

Oval

Submarine

Gift

Rectangle

Book

Truck

17

Lightning McQueen

In Cars, *Lightning McQueen is a hotshot rookie race car who cares only about two things: winning and the fame and fortune that come with it. But all of that changes when he suddenly finds himself in the sleepy old town of Radiator Springs. In Cars 2, Lightning is a worldwide celebrity whose every dream has come true. Famous, successful, and surrounded by great friends, Lightning is ready to enjoy time in the slow lane—just as soon as he wins the World Grand Prix.*

Step 1

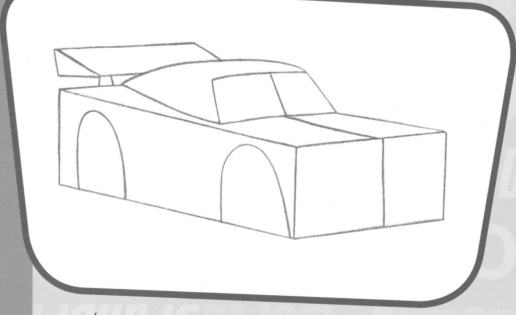

while he's competing in the races of the World Grand Prix, Lightning sports this tribute to Doc Hudson on his hood

Step 2

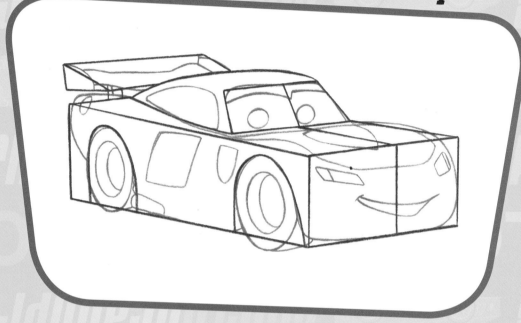

Lightning McQueen

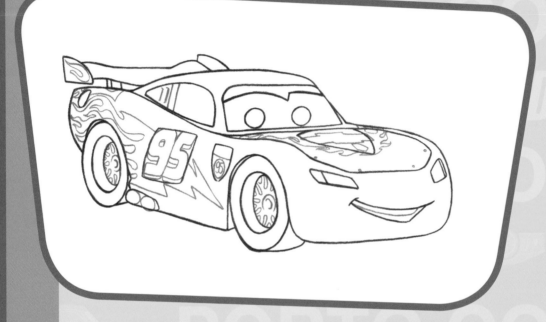

Step 3

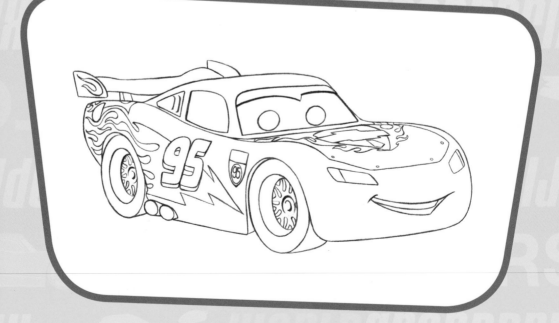

Step 4

for the WGP races,
Lightning gets a new,
sportier spoiler!

Mater

Mater is a friendly tow truck with a big heart, and he's always willing to lend a helping hook. He is the self-proclaimed world's best backward driver, who also gets a kick out of tractor tipping. In Cars 2, Mater gets caught up in a web of espionage when he accompanies Lightning to the World Grand Prix.

Step 1

YES!
mirrors are at irregular angles

NO!
mirrors are not perfectly aligned

Step 2

YES!   NO!

his misshapen buckteeth aren't
perfect squares—and there's a
gap between them

keep facial expressions
off center to emphasize
Mater's goofiness

YES!   YES!

NO!
too centered

Step 4

Sally

In Cars, Sally, a smart and beautiful sports car, is determined to restore Radiator Springs to the bustling town it was in its heyday. Originally an attorney from Los Angeles, she shows Lightning that sometimes it's good to live life in the slow lane. In Cars 2, Sally shows Lightning her support by showing up for the final leg of the World Grand Prix.

Step 1

Sally's eyebrows are heaviest at the peaks

YES!

NO!

Step 2

Step 3

Sally is just about a tire width
smaller than Lightning

Step 4

YES!
spokes
have
curved
pattern

NO!
not
straight

NO!
not
sharp

Doc Hudson

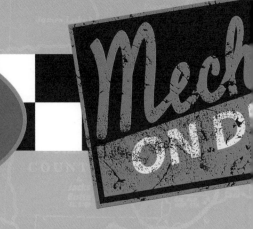

Doc is a respected and admired town doctor, and he's the judge in Radiator Springs. But he has a mysterious past. Protective of the town, Doc cherishes the quiet and simple life. He wants nothing to do with the flashy race car Lightning McQueen.

STEP 1

NO!

YES!

centerline helps transform
Doc's windshield into glasses

STEP 2

STEP 3

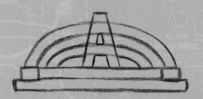

Doc's grille is like a rainbow built over the central letter A

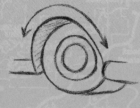

NO!
front fender isn't round

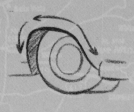

YES!
fender curves into front bumper

STEP 4

Sheriff

Sheriff is the keeper of the peace in Radiator Springs, and he takes his job very seriously. He enjoys telling stories about his beloved Mother Road, and he especially loves taking naps behind the Radiator Springs billboard.

STEP 1

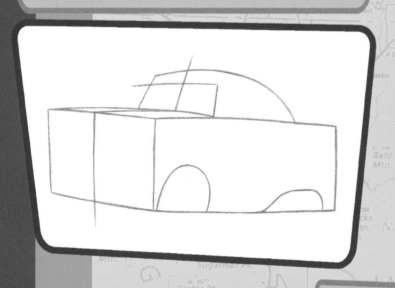

Sheriff's rounded, heavy body is shaped like a cream-filled donut

STEP 2

STEP 3

Sheriff's grille resembles a big, bushy moustache

STEP 4

Sheriff's big, red light is shaped like a dome

Red

Despite being a big, strong fire engine, Red is very shy and sensitive. If he's not cheerfully helping out his neighbors, you can find him lovingly tending to his flower garden.

STEP 1

YES!

NO!

eyelids show Red is shy—not aggressive

STEP 2

STEP 3

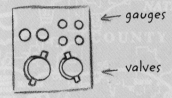
← gauges

← valves

valves can turn

STEP 4

front   back

Red's wheel curves
out from front tire
but is hidden within
rear tires

33

Ramone

Ramone loves to cruise low and slow—and to look good doing it. The owner of the local custom paint and body shop, Ramone is a paint artist extraordinaire. He enjoys trying on cool new looks by re-painting himself almost every day.

STEP 1

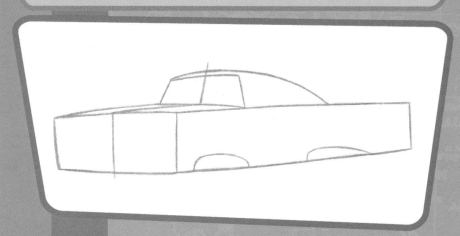

eyebrows make a "v" at the center

YES!

NO!

STEP 2

STEP 3

keep flames interesting and
varied—not too uniform

YES!

NO!

STEP 4

35

Flo

Flo is a sassy, no-nonsense show car with a big heart. Married to Ramone, she runs the local diner, where she serves the "finest fuel in 50 states."

STEP 1

NO! don't make tailfins too high

YES! top of fins are level with top of cab

STEP 2

STEP 3

YES!   NO!

Flo's eyelashes connect
like windshield wipers
and have thick peaks

STEP 4

YES!   NO!

NO!

top lip is long and
thin—bottom lip is
shorter and fatter

Luigi and Guido

Luigi is an Italian sports car who runs Casa Della Tires in Radiator Springs. Guido is an Italian forklift. In Cars 2, they volunteer to be in Lightning's pit crew at the World Grand Prix. They're thrilled that the second race in Porto Corsa, Italy is near their hometown!

Step 1

Step 2

NO!

not hard edges

YES!

edges are rounded

Step 1

Step 2

YES! head is wider at base

NO! head is not square

Fillmore and Sarge

Fillmore is a believer in all things natural. His "naturally" messy yard drives his neighbor Sarge, a patriotic veteran, absolutely nuts. Despite their constant bickering, they can't live without each other.

STEP 1

STEP 2

YES!

wheels close together and angle inward

NO!

wheels not far apart and evenly aligned

STEP 1

YES!

NO!

eyebrows more like window shades than windshield wipers

eyebrows don't curve

STEP 2

YES!   NO!

tires have tread

tires aren't slick like racing tires

The King

The King is a racing legend who has won more Piston Cups than any other car in history, but he manages to keep his priorities straight. He knows that it takes more than trophies to be a true champion.

PISTON

STEP 1

spoiler is same height as distance from the trunk to ground

STEP 2

NO! The King's front hood is pointed, not rounded

STEP 3

STEP 4

43

Chick

Chick is a racing veteran with a chip on his shoulder. He's a ruthless competitor who is notorious for cheating his way to second place. Always a runner-up, he'll do anything to win.

STEP 1

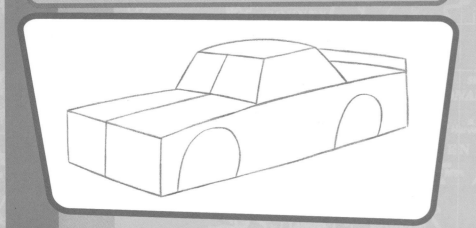

YES!

tires are big and wide

NO!

not too thin

STEP 2

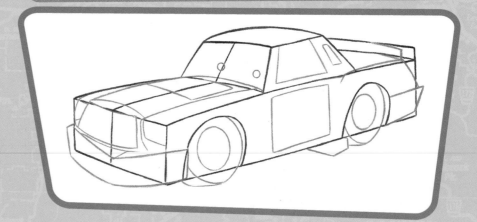

STEP 3

YES!

NO!

Chick has beady pupils and a sharp peak between his eyes

STEP 4

Chick considers himself prime real estate and is covered with sponsor stickers—so get creative with sticker shapes and placement

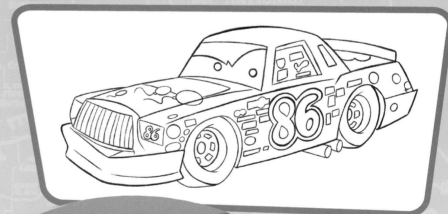

45

Finn McMissile

British Agent Finn McMissile is sleek, charming, intelligent, and loaded with cool gadgets! Finn knows there's a conspiracy afoot at the World Grand Prix. With the help of fellow British Agent Holley Shiftwell—and Mater—he and his colleagues are destined to uncover the plot.

Step 1

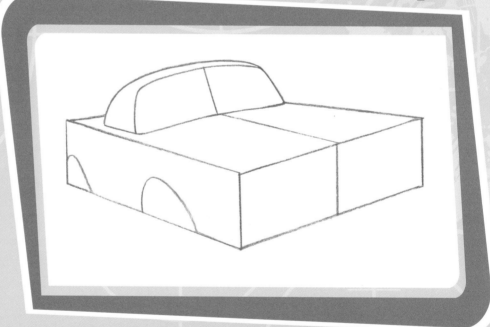

Finn has a built-in missile launcher and can fire grappling hooks

when his pupils are slightly covered by his eyelids, it conveys how cool he looks

Step 2

Step 3

Finn can transform into a hydroplane

Step 4

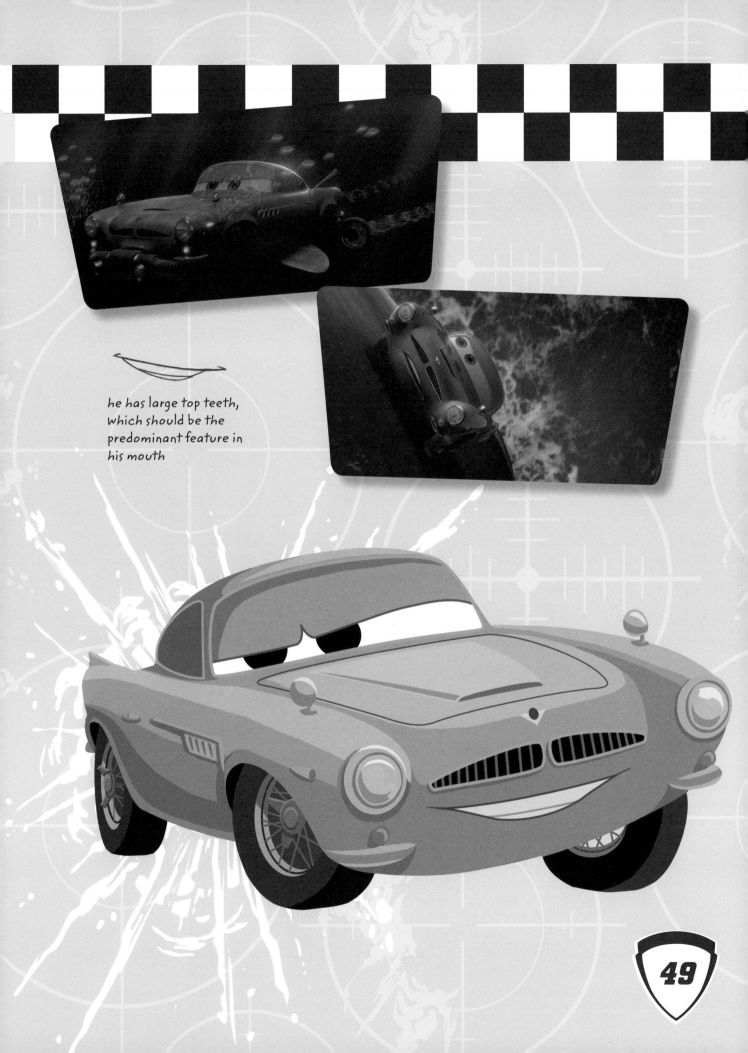

he has large top teeth, which should be the predominant feature in his mouth

Holley Shiftwell

Beautiful, young agent-in-training Holley Shiftwell knows all the standard operating procedures of top-secret work—and she knows how to follow them! Fresh out of the Academy, Holley gets her on-the-job field training by working to solve the World Grand Prix conspiracy with veteran Agent Finn McMissile.

Step 1

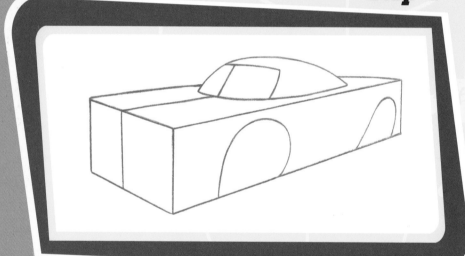

Holley has secret weapons, such as wings

Step 2

from the side, Holley can be constructed from smooth interlocking shapes with almost no sharp angles

Step 3

Holley has full lips

NO!
too simple

NO!
too thin

YES!

Holley has a screen that projects from her front turn indicators

Step 4

51

Francesco Bernoulli

International racing champ Francesco Bernoulli loves a good, clean race—almost as much as he adores himself. Francesco challenges Lightning McQueen to participate in the World Grand Prix. He even wins the first leg! Arrivederci!

Step 1

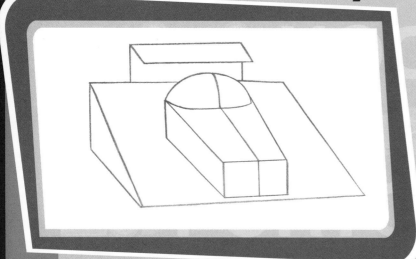

Francesco's "head" works like a helmet sitting down into the body with the air intake above

Step 2

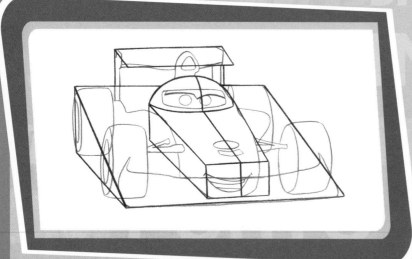

YES!

NO!

because his mouth is so far away from his eyes, his expressions will read more easily when he's turned more toward us rather than to the side

Step 3

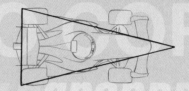

his basic body shape is a wedge that slices through the air for maximum speed!

Step 4

Francesco sits lower to the ground than Lightning

53

Professor Z

The smart and savvy mad scientist Professor Z has mastered the art of sophisticated weapons design and has created an elaborate device disguised as a camera that can harm cars without leaving a trace of evidence. His goal is to sabotage the World Grand Prix racers. Will he succeed?

Step 1

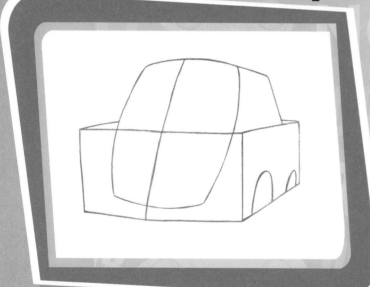

Professor Z is really small

Professor Z looks the same coming or going!

Step 2

his broken roof rack gives the appearance of a hair comb-over

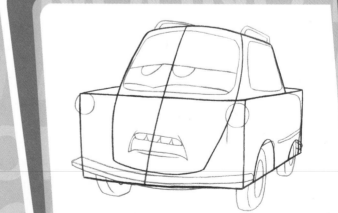

WGP

Step 3

be careful when
posing Professor Z
that his body angle
doesn't cause his eye
to be cut across by
his monocle

YES!

NO!

Step 4

Acer

Acer is one of Professor Z's main goons who carries out all of his dirty work. This Lemon, along with his buddy Grem, enjoys taking out the World Grand Prix racers one by one by aiming the TV camera device at them while they're zooming down the racetrack.

Step 1

NO! not too short

YES! Acer has a tall cab

Step 2

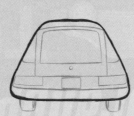
keep body shape simple, boxy, and soft

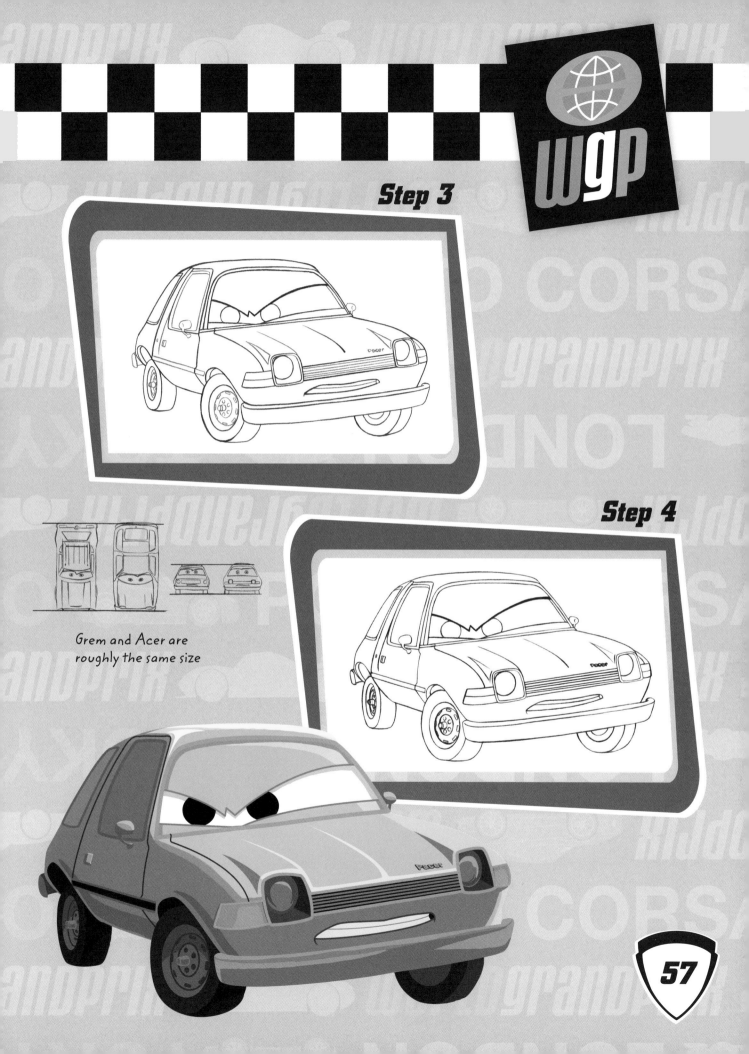

WGP

Step 3

Step 4

Grem and Acer are
roughly the same size

57

Grem

Grem is another of Professor Z's goons. Grem and his partner-in-crime, Acer, don't have the fancy gadgets that the spy cars have. But they are tough and relentless. They'll do anything to stop the secret agents!

Step 1

Grem has a distinctive decal on his side that resembles a hockey stick

Step 2

draw lower eyelids to make his expressions more shifty

from behind, his body shape looks like an upside-down cup on a saucer

Step 3

his front grille looks like a moustache, and he's missing some teeth because he's been in some fights

Step 4

when they're doing their dirty work, Grem and Acer are in contact with their boss by wearing headsets

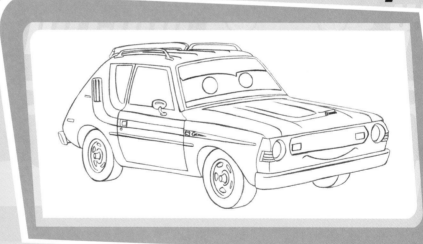

Miles Axlerod

Sir Miles Axlerod has devoted his life and fortune—acquired as an oil baron—to creating a renewable, alternative fuel called Allinol, which he showcases at a three-country race called the World Grand Prix. But Mater and his friends soon discover that Allinol isn't all it's cracked up to be—and neither is Axlerod.

Step 1

he has a very boxy appearance from the front

Step 2

Step 3

a winch on the back
carries his electrical plug

Step 4

the top of his cab
should resemble an
English driving cap

Siddeley

Whenever Finn McMissile is in a tight situation, Siddeley is there to bail him out! This super sleek British spy plane is equipped with weapons, gadgetry, computers, surveillance equipment, and much more. Siddeley is a top-notch spy who always travels in style.

Step 1

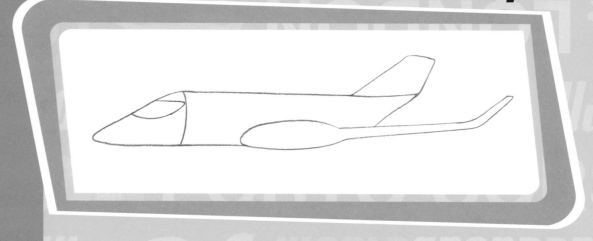

Step 2

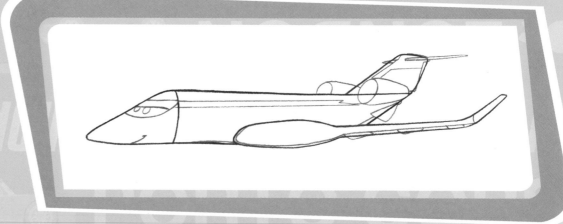

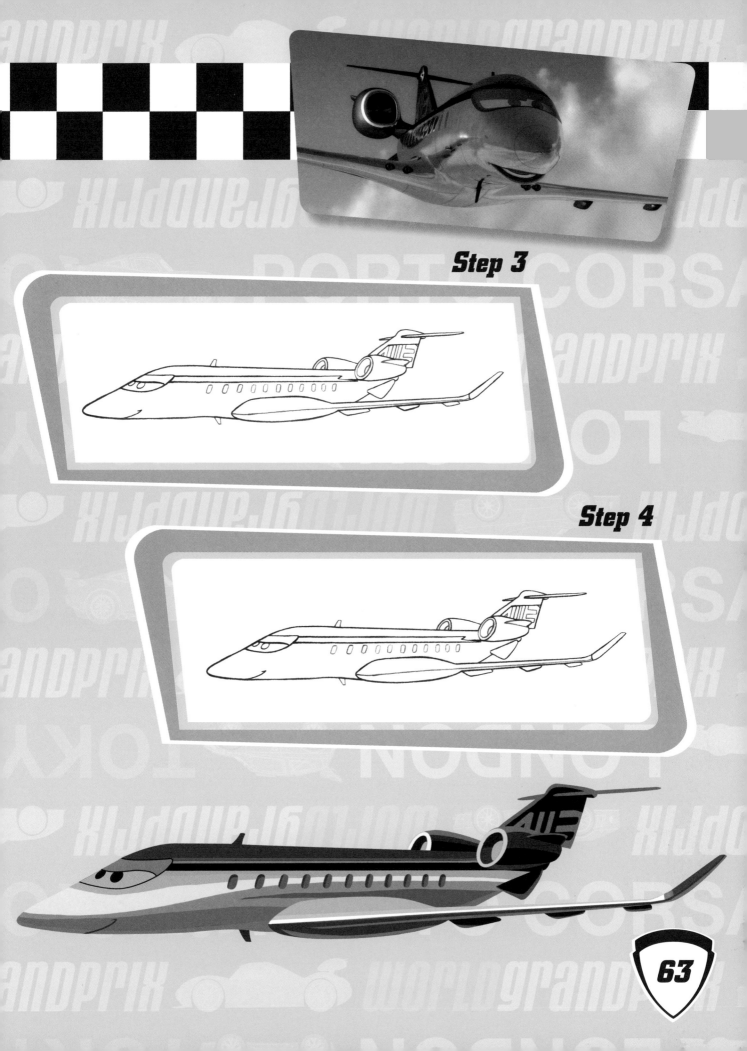

Step 3

Step 4

FRIENDSHIP—KA-CHOW!

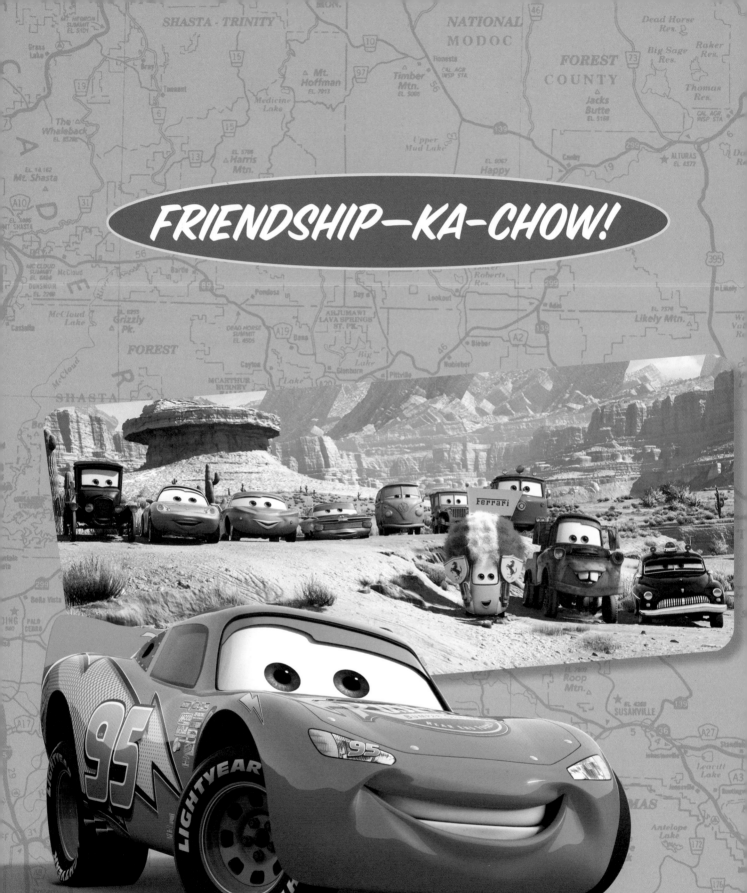